Sacred Soul

GRATITUDE JOURNAL

Introduction

Welcome, Friends!

If you find yourself with this journal in your hands, you're either a person who journals regularly—or, you're looking for change, hoping this journal will be it. Whatever your circumstances, I'll tell you this—you're going to get out of this life what you put into it. If you want change? Create it. Feeling unhappy? Find joy. Think there's something more out there? There is! Go find it, my friend.

This journal is a tool for you! In this life, we're born equipped with all we need inside of us. However, when we're born, all of that Divine knowledge is stripped away. We need to find—and, recognize—the tools in this life to help get us back on our path to enlightenment. And, that's the purpose of this gratitude journal—when you focus on things for which you're grateful, you'll find more reasons to be thankful. You'll also replace negative thoughts with positive thoughts and, it's through these steps, you'll experience change in your life.

The necessary steps? Committing time to yourself—but, I admit, finding time to make myself a priority is still hard for me. As a busy wife, mom, psychic medium, healer, author, and teacher, I know first hand about short hours in the day. And, as a spiritual leader, I know how important it is to value those hours to find time for you! Remember—you're important!

Make yourself a priority!

Dedication

It's with the most heartfelt gratitude I acknowledge my most beautiful gifts in this life—my children, Brooke Lynn, and Hunter Kenneth. There was a time I didn't know if children would be on my path, yet I always knew I was meant to be a mother—I just didn't realize it was according to the Divine's timing.

Your arrivals into my life have forever changed me for the good for you are my greatest teachers, and greatest blessings. I'll forever be thankful you were sent to be in my life—you give me inspiration to be better. To do better.

To live better.

Love,

Mom

"If ever there is a tomorrow when we're not together—there is something you must always remember. You are braver than you believe, stronger than you seem, and smarter than you think. But, the most important thing is even if we're apart, I'll always be with you."

—WINNIE THE POOH

"At times, our own light goes out, and is rekindled by a spark from another person. Each of us has cause to think with deep gratitude of those who have lighted the flame within us . . ."

—Albert Schweitzer

Gratitude to Fill Your Soul!

I AM THANKFUL FOR . . .   DATE _____

1. _____

2. _____

3. _____

I AM THANKFUL FOR . . .   DATE _____

1. _____

2. _____

3. _____

I AM THANKFUL FOR . . .   DATE _____

1. _____

2. _____

3 _____

"Acknowledging the good you already have in your
life is the foundation for all abundance."

—ECKHART TOLLE

Thoughts from Your Soul

Gratitude to Fill Your Soul!

I AM THANKFUL FOR . . .   DATE _____

1. _____

2. _____

3. _____

I AM THANKFUL FOR . . .   DATE _____

1. _____

2. _____

3. _____

I AM THANKFUL FOR . . .   DATE _____

1. _____

2. _____

3 _____

"Every time you smile at someone, it is an action of love, a gift to that person, a beautiful thing."

—MOTHER TERESA

Thoughts from Your Soul

Gratitude to Fill Your Soul!

I AM THANKFUL FOR . . .   DATE _____

1. _____

2. _____

3. _____

I AM THANKFUL FOR . . .   DATE _____

1. _____

2. _____

3. _____

I AM THANKFUL FOR . . .   DATE _____

1. _____

2. _____

3 _____

"This is a wonderful day—I've never seen it before."

—Maya Angelou

Thoughts from Your Soul

Gratitude to Fill Your Soul!

I AM THANKFUL FOR . . .   DATE _____

1. _____

2. _____

3. _____

I AM THANKFUL FOR . . .   DATE _____

1. _____

2. _____

3. _____

I AM THANKFUL FOR . . .   DATE _____

1. _____

2. _____

3 _____

*"When I started counting my blessings,
my whole life turned around."*

—WILLIE NELSON

Thoughts from Your Soul

Gratitude to Fill Your Soul!

I AM THANKFUL FOR . . .   DATE _____

1. _____

2. _____

3. _____

I AM THANKFUL FOR . . .   DATE _____

1. _____

2. _____

3. _____

I AM THANKFUL FOR . . .   DATE _____

1. _____

2. _____

3 _____

"What you seek is seeking you."

—RUMI

Thoughts from Your Soul

Gratitude to Fill Your Soul!

I AM THANKFUL FOR . . .   DATE _____

1. _____

2. _____

3. _____

I AM THANKFUL FOR . . .   DATE _____

1. _____

2. _____

3. _____

I AM THANKFUL FOR . . .   DATE _____

1. _____

2. _____

3 _____

"The way to move out of judgment is to move into gratitude."

—NEALE DONALD WALSCH

Thoughts from Your Soul

_____

_____

_____

_____

_____

_____

_____

_____

_____

_____

_____

_____

_____

_____

_____

_____

_____

_____

Gratitude to Fill Your Soul!

I AM THANKFUL FOR . . .   DATE _____

1. _____

2. _____

3. _____

I AM THANKFUL FOR . . .   DATE _____

1. _____

2. _____

3. _____

I AM THANKFUL FOR . . .   DATE _____

1. _____

2. _____

3 _____

*"Gratitude opens the door to the power, the
wisdom, the creativity of the universe."*

—DEEPAK CHOPRA

Thoughts from Your Soul

Gratitude to Fill Your Soul!

I AM THANKFUL FOR . . .   DATE _____

1. _____

2. _____

3. _____

I AM THANKFUL FOR . . .   DATE _____

1. _____

2. _____

3. _____

I AM THANKFUL FOR . . .   DATE _____

1. _____

2. _____

3 _____

"This above all, to thine own self be true."

—WILLIAM SHAKESPEARE

Thoughts from Your Soul

Gratitude to Fill Your Soul!

I AM THANKFUL FOR . . .   DATE _____

1. _____

2. _____

3. _____

I AM THANKFUL FOR . . .   DATE _____

1. _____

2. _____

3. _____

I AM THANKFUL FOR . . .   DATE _____

1. _____

2. _____

3 _____

"At the end of the day, let there be no excuses,
no explanations, and no regrets."

—DR. STEVE MARABOLI

Thoughts from Your Soul

Gratitude to Fill Your Soul!

I AM THANKFUL FOR . . .   DATE _____

1. _____

2. _____

3. _____

I AM THANKFUL FOR . . .   DATE _____

1. _____

2. _____

3. _____

I AM THANKFUL FOR . . .   DATE _____

1. _____

2. _____

3 _____

*"The real gift of gratitude is the more grateful you
are, the more present you become."*

—ROBERT HOLDEN

Thoughts from Your Soul

Gratitude to Fill Your Soul!

I AM THANKFUL FOR . . .   DATE _____

1. _____

2. _____

3. _____

I AM THANKFUL FOR . . .   DATE _____

1. _____

2. _____

3. _____

I AM THANKFUL FOR . . .   DATE _____

1. _____

2. _____

3 _____

"If the only prayer you ever say is 'Thank you,'
that will be enough."

—ECKHART TOLLE

Thoughts from Your Soul

Gratitude to Fill Your Soul!

I AM THANKFUL FOR . . .   DATE _____

1. _____

2. _____

3. _____

I AM THANKFUL FOR . . .   DATE _____

1. _____

2. _____

3. _____

I AM THANKFUL FOR . . .   DATE _____

1. _____

2. _____

3 _____

"Gratitude makes sense of our past, brings peace for today, and creates a vision for tomorrow."

—MELODY BEATTIE

Thoughts from Your Soul

Gratitude to Fill Your Soul!

I AM THANKFUL FOR . . .   DATE _____

1. _____

2. _____

3. _____

I AM THANKFUL FOR . . .   DATE _____

1. _____

2. _____

3. _____

I AM THANKFUL FOR . . .   DATE _____

1. _____

2. _____

3 _____

*"If you change the way you look at things,
the things you look at change."*

—WAYNE DYER

Thoughts from Your Soul

Gratitude to Fill Your Soul!

I AM THANKFUL FOR . . .   DATE _____

1. _____

2. _____

3. _____

I AM THANKFUL FOR . . .   DATE _____

1. _____

2. _____

3. _____

I AM THANKFUL FOR . . .   DATE _____

1. _____

2. _____

3 _____

"Life isn't about finding yourself,
it is about creating yourself."

—GEORGE BERNARD SHAW

Thoughts from Your Soul

Gratitude to Fill Your Soul!

I AM THANKFUL FOR . . .   DATE _____

1. _____

2. _____

3. _____

I AM THANKFUL FOR . . .   DATE _____

1. _____

2. _____

3. _____

I AM THANKFUL FOR . . .   DATE _____

1. _____

2. _____

3 _____

"Gratitude is riches, complaint is poverty."

—DORIS DAY

Thoughts from Your Soul

Gratitude to Fill Your Soul!

I AM THANKFUL FOR . . .   DATE _____

1. _____

2. _____

3. _____

I AM THANKFUL FOR . . .   DATE _____

1. _____

2. _____

3. _____

I AM THANKFUL FOR . . .   DATE _____

1. _____

2. _____

3 _____

*"It is not joy that makes us grateful,
it is gratitude that makes us joyful."*

—BROTHER DAVID STEINDL-RAST

Thoughts from Your Soul

Gratitude to Fill Your Soul!

I AM THANKFUL FOR . . .   DATE _____

1. _____

2. _____

3. _____

I AM THANKFUL FOR . . .   DATE _____

1. _____

2. _____

3. _____

I AM THANKFUL FOR . . .   DATE _____

1. _____

2. _____

3 _____

*"So much has been given to me, I have no time to
ponder over that which has been denied."*

—HELEN KELLER

Thoughts from Your Soul

Gratitude to Fill Your Soul!

I AM THANKFUL FOR . . .   DATE _____

1. _____

2. _____

3. _____

I AM THANKFUL FOR . . .   DATE _____

1. _____

2. _____

3. _____

I AM THANKFUL FOR . . .   DATE _____

1. _____

2. _____

3 _____

"Surrender to what is. Let go of what was.
Have faith in what will be."

—SONIA RICOTTI

Thoughts from Your Soul

Gratitude to Fill Your Soul!

I AM THANKFUL FOR . . . DATE _____

1. _____

2. _____

3. _____

I AM THANKFUL FOR . . . DATE _____

1. _____

2. _____

3. _____

I AM THANKFUL FOR . . . DATE _____

1. _____

2. _____

3 _____

*"Happiness is when what you think, what you
say, and what you do are in harmony."*

—MAHATMA GHANDI

Thoughts from Your Soul

Gratitude to Fill Your Soul!

I AM THANKFUL FOR . . .   DATE _____

1. _____

2. _____

3. _____

I AM THANKFUL FOR . . .   DATE _____

1. _____

2. _____

3. _____

I AM THANKFUL FOR . . .   DATE _____

1. _____

2. _____

3 _____

"See the light in others,
and treat them as if that's all you see."

—WAYNE DYER

Thoughts from Your Soul

Gratitude to Fill Your Soul!

I AM THANKFUL FOR . . .   DATE _____

1. _____

2. _____

3. _____

I AM THANKFUL FOR . . .   DATE _____

1. _____

2. _____

3. _____

I AM THANKFUL FOR . . .   DATE _____

1. _____

2. _____

3 _____

"Happiness cannot be traveled to, owned, earned, worn, or consumed. Happiness is the spiritual experience of living every minute with love, grace, and gratitude."

—DENIS WAITLEY

Thoughts from Your Soul

Gratitude to Fill Your Soul!

I AM THANKFUL FOR . . .   DATE _____

1. _____

2. _____

3. _____

I AM THANKFUL FOR . . .   DATE _____

1. _____

2. _____

3. _____

I AM THANKFUL FOR . . .   DATE _____

1. _____

2. _____

3 _____

*"Happiness or sorrow—whatever befalls you,
walk on untouched, unattached."*

—BUDDHA

Thoughts from Your Soul

Gratitude to Fill Your Soul!

I AM THANKFUL FOR . . .   DATE _____

1. _____

2. _____

3. _____

I AM THANKFUL FOR . . .   DATE _____

1. _____

2. _____

3. _____

I AM THANKFUL FOR . . .   DATE _____

1. _____

2. _____

3 _____

"Only I can change my life.
No one can do it for me."

—CAROL BURNETT

Thoughts from Your Soul

Gratitude to Fill Your Soul!

I AM THANKFUL FOR . . .   DATE _____

1. _____

2. _____

3. _____

I AM THANKFUL FOR . . .   DATE _____

1. _____

2. _____

3. _____

I AM THANKFUL FOR . . .   DATE _____

1. _____

2. _____

3 _____

*"Be thankful for what you have—you'll end up having
more. If you concentrate on what you don't have,
you will never, ever have enough."*

—OPRAH WINFREY

Thoughts from Your Soul

Gratitude to Fill Your Soul!

I AM THANKFUL FOR . . . DATE _____

1. _____

2. _____

3. _____

I AM THANKFUL FOR . . . DATE _____

1. _____

2. _____

3. _____

I AM THANKFUL FOR . . . DATE _____

1. _____

2. _____

3 _____

"It's not about how much you do, but how much love
you put into what you do that counts."

—MOTHER TERESA

Thoughts from Your Soul

Gratitude to Fill Your Soul!

I AM THANKFUL FOR . . .   DATE _____

1. _____

2. _____

3. _____

I AM THANKFUL FOR . . .   DATE _____

1. _____

2. _____

3. _____

I AM THANKFUL FOR . . .   DATE _____

1. _____

2. _____

3 _____

"Reflect upon your present blessings of which every man has plenty—
not only your past misfortunes of which all men have some."

—CHARLES DICKENS

Thoughts from Your Soul

Gratitude to Fill Your Soul!

I AM THANKFUL FOR . . .   DATE _____

1. _____

2. _____

3. _____

I AM THANKFUL FOR . . .   DATE _____

1. _____

2. _____

3. _____

I AM THANKFUL FOR . . .   DATE _____

1. _____

2. _____

3 _____

"The path to love is our spiritual destiny."

—DEEPAK CHOPRA

Thoughts from Your Soul

Gratitude to Fill Your Soul!

I AM THANKFUL FOR . . .   DATE _____

1. _____

2. _____

3. _____

I AM THANKFUL FOR . . .   DATE _____

1. _____

2. _____

3. _____

I AM THANKFUL FOR . . .   DATE _____

1. _____

2. _____

3 _____

"Learn from yesterday,
live for today,
hope for tomorrow."

—ALBERT EINSTEIN

Thoughts from Your Soul

Gratitude to Fill Your Soul!

I AM THANKFUL FOR . . .   DATE _____

1. _____

2. _____

3. _____

I AM THANKFUL FOR . . .   DATE _____

1. _____

2. _____

3. _____

I AM THANKFUL FOR . . .   DATE _____

1. _____

2. _____

3 _____

"The inspiration you seek is already within you.
Be silent, and listen."

—RUMI

Thoughts from Your Soul

Gratitude to Fill Your Soul!

I AM THANKFUL FOR . . .   DATE _____

1. _____

2. _____

3. _____

I AM THANKFUL FOR . . .   DATE _____

1. _____

2. _____

3. _____

I AM THANKFUL FOR . . .   DATE _____

1. _____

2. _____

3 _____

*"When we focus on our gratitude, the tide of disappointment
goes out, and the tide of love rushes in."*

—KRISTIN ARMSTRONG

Thoughts from Your Soul

Gratitude to Fill Your Soul!

I AM THANKFUL FOR . . .   DATE _____

1. _____

2. _____

3. _____

I AM THANKFUL FOR . . .   DATE _____

1. _____

2. _____

3. _____

I AM THANKFUL FOR . . .   DATE _____

1. _____

2. _____

3 _____

"Abundance is not something we acquire,
it is something we tune in to."

—WAYNE DYER

Thoughts from Your Soul

Gratitude to Fill Your Soul!

I AM THANKFUL FOR . . .   DATE _____

1. _____

2. _____

3. _____

I AM THANKFUL FOR . . .   DATE _____

1. _____

2. _____

3. _____

I AM THANKFUL FOR . . .   DATE _____

1. _____

2. _____

3 _____

"People take different roads seeking fulfillment and happiness.
Just because they are not on your road
does not mean they are lost."

—DALAI LAMA

Thoughts from Your Soul

Gratitude to Fill Your Soul!

I AM THANKFUL FOR . . .   DATE _____

1. _____

2. _____

3. _____

I AM THANKFUL FOR . . .   DATE _____

1. _____

2. _____

3. _____

I AM THANKFUL FOR . . .   DATE _____

1. _____

2. _____

3 _____

"The more you praise and celebrate your life,
the more there is in life to celebrate."

—OPRAH WINFREY

Thoughts from Your Soul

Gratitude to Fill Your Soul!

I AM THANKFUL FOR . . .   DATE _____

1. _____

2. _____

3. _____

I AM THANKFUL FOR . . .   DATE _____

1. _____

2. _____

3. _____

I AM THANKFUL FOR . . .   DATE _____

1. _____

2. _____

3 _____

"The most beautiful things in the world cannot be seen, or even touched. They must be felt with the heart."

—HELEN KELLER

Thoughts from Your Soul

Gratitude to Fill Your Soul!

I AM THANKFUL FOR . . .   DATE _____

1. _____

2. _____

3. _____

I AM THANKFUL FOR . . .   DATE _____

1. _____

2. _____

3. _____

I AM THANKFUL FOR . . .   DATE _____

1. _____

2. _____

3 _____

"Wear gratitude like a cloak,
and it will feed every corner of your life."

—RUMI

Thoughts from Your Soul

Gratitude to Fill Your Soul!

I AM THANKFUL FOR . . .   DATE _____

1. _____

2. _____

3. _____

I AM THANKFUL FOR . . .   DATE _____

1. _____

2. _____

3. _____

I AM THANKFUL FOR . . .   DATE _____

1. _____

2. _____

3 _____

"Gratitude turns what we have into enough."

—MELODY BEATTIE

Thoughts from Your Soul

Gratitude to Fill Your Soul!

I AM THANKFUL FOR . . .   DATE _____

1. _____

2. _____

3. _____

I AM THANKFUL FOR . . .   DATE _____

1. _____

2. _____

3. _____

I AM THANKFUL FOR . . .   DATE _____

1. _____

2. _____

3 _____

*"The miracle of gratitude is that it shifts your perception
to such an extent, it changes the world you see."*

—DR. ROBERT HOLDEN

Thoughts from Your Soul

Gratitude to Fill Your Soul!

I AM THANKFUL FOR . . .   DATE _____

1. _____

2. _____

3. _____

I AM THANKFUL FOR . . .   DATE _____

1. _____

2. _____

3. _____

I AM THANKFUL FOR . . .   DATE _____

1. _____

2. _____

3 _____

*"Love is such a deep gratitude. When you are truly in
love with life, every breath you take is gratitude."*

—BRYANT MCGILL

Thoughts from Your Soul

Gratitude to Fill Your Soul!

I AM THANKFUL FOR . . .   DATE _____

1. _____

2. _____

3. _____

I AM THANKFUL FOR . . .   DATE _____

1. _____

2. _____

3. _____

I AM THANKFUL FOR . . .   DATE _____

1. _____

2. _____

3 _____

"Feeling gratitude and not expressing it is like
wrapping a present, and not giving it."

—WILLIAM ARTHUR WARD

Thoughts from Your Soul

Gratitude to Fill Your Soul!

I AM THANKFUL FOR . . .   DATE _____

1. _____

2. _____

3. _____

I AM THANKFUL FOR . . .   DATE _____

1. _____

2. _____

3. _____

I AM THANKFUL FOR . . .   DATE _____

1. _____

2. _____

3 _____

"Enjoy the little things for one day you may look
back, and realize they were the big things."

—ROBERT BRAULT

Thoughts from Your Soul

Gratitude to Fill Your Soul!

I AM THANKFUL FOR . . .   DATE _____

1. _____

2. _____

3. _____

I AM THANKFUL FOR . . .   DATE _____

1. _____

2. _____

3. _____

I AM THANKFUL FOR . . .   DATE _____

1. _____

2. _____

3 _____

*"Trade your expectations for appreciation, and
your whole world changes in an instant."*

—TONY ROBBINS

Thoughts from Your Soul

_____

_____

_____

_____

_____

_____

_____

_____

_____

_____

_____

_____

_____

_____

_____

_____

_____

Gratitude to Fill Your Soul!

I AM THANKFUL FOR . . .   DATE _____

1. _____

2. _____

3. _____

I AM THANKFUL FOR . . .   DATE _____

1. _____

2. _____

3. _____

I AM THANKFUL FOR . . .   DATE _____

1. _____

2. _____

3 _____

*"Gratitude bestows reverence, allowing us to encounter every
day epiphanies . . . those transcendent moments of awe that
change forever how we experience life and the world."*

—JOHN MILTON

Thoughts from Your Soul

Gratitude to Fill Your Soul!

I AM THANKFUL FOR . . .   DATE _____

1. _____

2. _____

3. _____

I AM THANKFUL FOR . . .   DATE _____

1. _____

2. _____

3. _____

I AM THANKFUL FOR . . .   DATE _____

1. _____

2. _____

3 _____

"What separates privilege from entitlement is gratitude."

—BRENE BROWN

Thoughts from Your Soul

Gratitude to Fill Your Soul!

I AM THANKFUL FOR . . .   DATE _____

1. _____

2. _____

3. _____

I AM THANKFUL FOR . . .   DATE _____

1. _____

2. _____

3. _____

I AM THANKFUL FOR . . .   DATE _____

1. _____

2. _____

3 _____

"Gratitude is an essential part of being present. When you go
deeply into the present, gratitude arises spontaneously."

—ECKHART TOLLE

Thoughts from Your Soul

Gratitude to Fill Your Soul!

I AM THANKFUL FOR . . .   DATE _____

1. _____

2. _____

3. _____

I AM THANKFUL FOR . . .   DATE _____

1. _____

2. _____

3. _____

I AM THANKFUL FOR . . .   DATE _____

1. _____

2. _____

3 _____

"As we express our gratitude, we must never forget the highest appreciation is not to utter words, but to live by them."

—JOHN F. KENNEDY

Thoughts from Your Soul

Gratitude to Fill Your Soul!

I AM THANKFUL FOR . . .   DATE _____

1. _____

2. _____

3. _____

I AM THANKFUL FOR . . .   DATE _____

1. _____

2. _____

3. _____

I AM THANKFUL FOR . . .   DATE _____

1. _____

2. _____

3 _____

*"Let us be grateful to the people who make us happy—they are
the charming gardeners who make our souls blossom."*

—MARCEL PROUST

Thoughts from Your Soul

Gratitude to Fill Your Soul!

I AM THANKFUL FOR . . .   DATE _____

1. _____

2. _____

3. _____

I AM THANKFUL FOR . . .   DATE _____

1. _____

2. _____

3. _____

I AM THANKFUL FOR . . .   DATE _____

1. _____

2. _____

3 _____

"Walk as if you are kissing the Earth with your feet."

—THICH NHAT HANH

Thoughts from Your Soul

Gratitude to Fill Your Soul!

I AM THANKFUL FOR . . .   DATE _____

1. _____

2. _____

3. _____

I AM THANKFUL FOR . . .   DATE _____

1. _____

2. _____

3. _____

I AM THANKFUL FOR . . .   DATE _____

1. _____

2. _____

3 _____

"Be mindful. Be grateful. Be positive. Be true. Be kind."

—ROY T. BENNETT

Thoughts from Your Soul

Gratitude to Fill Your Soul!

I AM THANKFUL FOR . . .   DATE _____

1. _____

2. _____

3. _____

I AM THANKFUL FOR . . .   DATE _____

1. _____

2. _____

3. _____

I AM THANKFUL FOR . . .   DATE _____

1. _____

2. _____

3 _____

"Do not spoil what you have by desiring what you have not—remember
what you now have was once among the things you only hoped for."

—EPICURUS

Thoughts from Your Soul

Gratitude to Fill Your Soul!

I AM THANKFUL FOR . . .   DATE _____

1. _____

2. _____

3. _____

I AM THANKFUL FOR . . .   DATE _____

1. _____

2. _____

3. _____

I AM THANKFUL FOR . . .   DATE _____

1. _____

2. _____

3 _____

"We can complain because rose bushes have thorns,
or rejoice because thorns have roses."

—ALPHONSE KARR

Thoughts from Your Soul

Gratitude to Fill Your Soul!

I AM THANKFUL FOR . . .   DATE _____

1. _____

2. _____

3. _____

I AM THANKFUL FOR . . .   DATE _____

1. _____

2. _____

3. _____

I AM THANKFUL FOR . . .   DATE _____

1. _____

2. _____

3 _____

*"You can never cross the ocean unless you are
brave enough to lose sight of the shore."*

—CHRISTOPHER COLUMBUS

Thoughts from Your Soul

Gratitude to Fill Your Soul!

I AM THANKFUL FOR . . .   DATE _____

1. _____

2. _____

3. _____

I AM THANKFUL FOR . . .   DATE _____

1. _____

2. _____

3. _____

I AM THANKFUL FOR . . .   DATE _____

1. _____

2. _____

3 _____

"I am only one, but still I am one. I cannot do everything, but still I can do something. And, because I cannot do everything, I will not refuse to do the something I can do."

—HELLEN KELLER

Thoughts from Your Soul

Gratitude to Fill Your Soul!

I AM THANKFUL FOR . . .   DATE _____

1. _____

2. _____

3. _____

I AM THANKFUL FOR . . .   DATE _____

1. _____

2. _____

3. _____

I AM THANKFUL FOR . . .   DATE _____

1. _____

2. _____

3 _____

*"True forgiveness is when you can say,
'Thank you for that experience.'"*

—OPRAH WINFREY

Thoughts from Your Soul

Gratitude to Fill Your Soul!

I AM THANKFUL FOR . . .   DATE _____

1. _____

2. _____

3. _____

I AM THANKFUL FOR . . .   DATE _____

1. _____

2. _____

3. _____

I AM THANKFUL FOR . . .   DATE _____

1. _____

2. _____

3 _____

*"Always remember people who have helped you along
the way, and don't forget to lift someone up."*

—ROY T. BENNETT

Thoughts from Your Soul

Gratitude to Fill Your Soul!

I AM THANKFUL FOR . . .   DATE _____

1. _____

2. _____

3. _____

I AM THANKFUL FOR . . .   DATE _____

1. _____

2. _____

3. _____

I AM THANKFUL FOR . . .   DATE _____

1. _____

2. _____

3 _____

"At the end of the day, let there be no excuses,
no explanations, no regrets."

—STEVE MARABOLI

Thoughts from Your Soul

Gratitude to Fill Your Soul!

I AM THANKFUL FOR . . .   DATE _____

1. _____

2. _____

3. _____

I AM THANKFUL FOR . . .   DATE _____

1. _____

2. _____

3. _____

I AM THANKFUL FOR . . .   DATE _____

1. _____

2. _____

3 _____

"Let gratitude be the pillow upon which you kneel to say your nightly prayer. And, let faith be the bridge you build to overcome evil, and welcome good."

—MAYA ANGELOU

Thoughts from Your Soul

Gratitude to Fill Your Soul!

I AM THANKFUL FOR . . .　　　　DATE _____

1. _____

2. _____

3. _____

I AM THANKFUL FOR . . .　　　　DATE _____

1. _____

2. _____

3. _____

I AM THANKFUL FOR . . .　　　　DATE _____

1. _____

2. _____

3 _____

"In the end, though, maybe we must all give up trying to pay back the people in this world who sustain our lives. In the end, maybe it's wiser to surrender before the miraculous scope of human generosity, and to keep saying thank you, forever and sincerely, for as long as we have voices."

—ELIZABETH GILBERT

Thoughts from Your Soul

Gratitude to Fill Your Soul!

I AM THANKFUL FOR . . .   DATE _____

1. _____

2. _____

3. _____

I AM THANKFUL FOR . . .   DATE _____

1. _____

2. _____

3. _____

I AM THANKFUL FOR . . .   DATE _____

1. _____

2. _____

3 _____

*"We must find time to stop and thank the people
who make a difference in our lives."*

—JOHN F. KENNEDY

Thoughts from Your Soul

Gratitude to Fill Your Soul!

I AM THANKFUL FOR . . .   DATE _____

1. _____

2. _____

3. _____

I AM THANKFUL FOR . . .   DATE _____

1. _____

2. _____

3. _____

I AM THANKFUL FOR . . .   DATE _____

1. _____

2. _____

3 _____

"You pray in your distress and in your need; would that you might pray
also in the fullness of your joy, and in your days of abundance."

—KAHILL GIBRAN

Thoughts from Your Soul

Gratitude to Fill Your Soul!

I AM THANKFUL FOR . . . DATE _____

1. _____

2. _____

3. _____

I AM THANKFUL FOR . . . DATE _____

1. _____

2. _____

3. _____

I AM THANKFUL FOR . . . DATE _____

1. _____

2. _____

3 _____

"When you arise in the morning, think of what a precious privilege it is to be alive—to breathe, to think, to enjoy, to love—then, make that day count."

—STEVE MARABOLI

Thoughts from Your Soul

Gratitude to Fill Your Soul!

I AM THANKFUL FOR . . .   DATE _____

1. _____

2. _____

3. _____

I AM THANKFUL FOR . . .   DATE _____

1. _____

2. _____

3. _____

I AM THANKFUL FOR . . .   DATE _____

1. _____

2. _____

3 _____

"Gratitude can transform common days into Thanksgivings, turn routine jobs into joy, and change ordinary opportunities into blessings."

—WILLIAM ARTHUR WARD

Thoughts from Your Soul

Gratitude to Fill Your Soul!

I AM THANKFUL FOR . . .   DATE _____

1. _____

2. _____

3. _____

I AM THANKFUL FOR . . .   DATE _____

1. _____

2. _____

3. _____

I AM THANKFUL FOR . . .   DATE _____

1. _____

2. _____

3 _____

*"The world is 3 days—as for yesterday, it has vanished
along with all that was in it. As for tomorrow, you may
never see it. As for today, it is yours, so work on it."*

—HASAN AL-BASRI

Thoughts from Your Soul

Gratitude to Fill Your Soul!

I AM THANKFUL FOR . . .   DATE _____

1. _____

2. _____

3. _____

I AM THANKFUL FOR . . .   DATE _____

1. _____

2. _____

3. _____

I AM THANKFUL FOR . . .   DATE _____

1. _____

2. _____

3 _____

"We don't see the things the way they are.
We see things the way WE are."

—TALMUND

Thoughts from Your Soul

Gratitude to Fill Your Soul!

I AM THANKFUL FOR . . .   DATE _____

1. _____

2. _____

3. _____

I AM THANKFUL FOR . . .   DATE _____

1. _____

2. _____

3. _____

I AM THANKFUL FOR . . .   DATE _____

1. _____

2. _____

3 _____

"The problem is not that there are problems. The problem is expecting otherwise, and thinking having problems is a problem."

—THEODORE RUBIN

Thoughts from Your Soul

Gratitude to Fill Your Soul!

I AM THANKFUL FOR . . .   DATE _____

1. _____

2. _____

3. _____

I AM THANKFUL FOR . . .   DATE _____

1. _____

2. _____

3. _____

I AM THANKFUL FOR . . .   DATE _____

1. _____

2. _____

3 _____

"Yesterday is history, tomorrow is a mystery. And, today?
Today is a gift. That's why we call it the present."

—B. OLATUNJI

Thoughts from Your Soul

Gratitude to Fill Your Soul!

I AM THANKFUL FOR . . .   DATE _____

1. _____

2. _____

3. _____

I AM THANKFUL FOR . . .   DATE _____

1. _____

2. _____

3. _____

I AM THANKFUL FOR . . .   DATE _____

1. _____

2. _____

3 _____

*"When you get to the end of the rope,
tie a knot and hang on."*

—FRANKLIN D. ROOSEVELT

Thoughts from Your Soul

Gratitude to Fill Your Soul!

I AM THANKFUL FOR . . .   DATE _____

1. _____

2. _____

3. _____

I AM THANKFUL FOR . . .   DATE _____

1. _____

2. _____

3. _____

I AM THANKFUL FOR . . .   DATE _____

1. _____

2. _____

3 _____

"Your attitude, not your aptitude, determines your altitude."

—Zig Ziglar

Thoughts from Your Soul

Gratitude to Fill Your Soul!

I AM THANKFUL FOR . . .   DATE _____

1. _____

2. _____

3. _____

I AM THANKFUL FOR . . .   DATE _____

1. _____

2. _____

3. _____

I AM THANKFUL FOR . . .   DATE _____

1. _____

2. _____

3 _____

"The miracle is not to walk on water. The miracle is to walk on the green earth, dwelling deeply in the present moment, and feeling truly alive."

—THICH NHAT HANH

Thoughts from Your Soul

Gratitude to Fill Your Soul!

I AM THANKFUL FOR . . .   DATE _____

1. _____

2. _____

3. _____

I AM THANKFUL FOR . . .   DATE _____

1. _____

2. _____

3. _____

I AM THANKFUL FOR . . .   DATE _____

1. _____

2. _____

3 _____

"The greatest wisdom is in simplicity. Love, respect, tolerance, sharing, gratitude, forgiveness. It's not complex or elaborate. The real knowledge is free. It's encoded in your DNA. All you need is within you. Great teachers have said that from the beginning. Find your heart, and you will find your way."

—CARLOS BARRIOS

Thoughts from Your Soul

Gratitude to Fill Your Soul!

I AM THANKFUL FOR . . .   DATE _____

1. _____

2. _____

3. _____

I AM THANKFUL FOR . . .   DATE _____

1. _____

2. _____

3. _____

I AM THANKFUL FOR . . .   DATE _____

1. _____

2. _____

3 _____

"Breath is the finest gift of nature.
Be grateful for this wonderful gift."

—AMIT RAY

Thoughts from Your Soul

Gratitude to Fill Your Soul!

I AM THANKFUL FOR . . .   DATE _____

1. _____

2. _____

3. _____

I AM THANKFUL FOR . . .   DATE _____

1. _____

2. _____

3. _____

I AM THANKFUL FOR . . .   DATE _____

1. _____

2. _____

3 _____

"There is strange comfort in knowing that no matter what
happens today, the sun will rise again tomorrow."

—AARON LAURITSEN

Thoughts from Your Soul

Gratitude to Fill Your Soul!

I AM THANKFUL FOR . . . DATE _____

1. _____

2. _____

3. _____

I AM THANKFUL FOR . . . DATE _____

1. _____

2. _____

3. _____

I AM THANKFUL FOR . . . DATE _____

1. _____

2. _____

3 _____

*"In ordinary life, we hardly realize we receive a great deal more
than we give, and it is only with gratitude life becomes rich."*

—Deitrich Bonhoeffer

Thoughts from Your Soul

Gratitude to Fill Your Soul!

I AM THANKFUL FOR . . .   DATE _____

1. _____

2. _____

3. _____

I AM THANKFUL FOR . . .   DATE _____

1. _____

2. _____

3. _____

I AM THANKFUL FOR . . .   DATE _____

1. _____

2. _____

3 _____

"I think real friendship always makes us feel such sweet gratitude—
because the world almost always seems like a very hard desert, and
the flowers that grow there seem to grow against such high odds."

—STEPHEN KING

Thoughts from Your Soul

Gratitude to Fill Your Soul!

I AM THANKFUL FOR . . .   DATE _____

1. _____

2. _____

3. _____

I AM THANKFUL FOR . . .   DATE _____

1. _____

2. _____

3. _____

I AM THANKFUL FOR . . .   DATE _____

1. _____

2. _____

3 _____

"The struggles we endure today will be the 'good
old days' we laugh about tomorrow."

—AARON LAURITSEN

Thoughts from Your Soul

Gratitude to Fill Your Soul!

I AM THANKFUL FOR . . .   DATE _____

1. _____

2. _____

3. _____

I AM THANKFUL FOR . . .   DATE _____

1. _____

2. _____

3. _____

I AM THANKFUL FOR . . .   DATE _____

1. _____

2. _____

3 _____

*I may not be where I want to be, but I'm thankful
for not being where I used to be.*

—HABEEB AKANDE

Thoughts from Your Soul

Gratitude to Fill Your Soul!

I AM THANKFUL FOR . . .   DATE _____

1. _____

2. _____

3. _____

I AM THANKFUL FOR . . .   DATE _____

1. _____

2. _____

3. _____

I AM THANKFUL FOR . . .   DATE _____

1. _____

2. _____

3 _____

*"Gratitude is the ability to experience life as a gift. It
liberates us from the prison of self-preoccupation."*

—JOHN ORTBERG

Thoughts from Your Soul

Gratitude to Fill Your Soul!

I AM THANKFUL FOR . . .   DATE _____

1. _____

2. _____

3. _____

I AM THANKFUL FOR . . .   DATE _____

1. _____

2. _____

3. _____

I AM THANKFUL FOR . . .   DATE _____

1. _____

2. _____

3 _____

*"Most of the important things in the world have been accomplished by
people who have kept on trying when there seemed to be no hope, at all."*

—DALE CARNEGIE

Thoughts from Your Soul

Gratitude to Fill Your Soul!

I AM THANKFUL FOR . . .   DATE _____

1. _____

2. _____

3. _____

I AM THANKFUL FOR . . .   DATE _____

1. _____

2. _____

3. _____

I AM THANKFUL FOR . . .   DATE _____

1. _____

2. _____

3 _____

"Our greatest glory is not in never failing,
but, in rising every time we fall."

—CONFUCIOUS

Thoughts from Your Soul

Gratitude to Fill Your Soul!

I AM THANKFUL FOR . . .   DATE _____

1. _____

2. _____

3. _____

I AM THANKFUL FOR . . .   DATE _____

1. _____

2. _____

3. _____

I AM THANKFUL FOR . . .   DATE _____

1. _____

2. _____

3 _____

*"So many of our dreams at first seem impossible, then
they seem improbable—and, then, when we summon
the will, they soon become inevitable."*

—CHRISTOPHER REEVE

Thoughts from Your Soul

_____

_____

_____

_____

_____

_____

_____

_____

_____

_____

_____

_____

_____

_____

_____

_____

_____

_____

Gratitude to Fill Your Soul!

I AM THANKFUL FOR . . .   DATE _____

1. _____

2. _____

3. _____

I AM THANKFUL FOR . . .   DATE _____

1. _____

2. _____

3. _____

I AM THANKFUL FOR . . .   DATE _____

1. _____

2. _____

3 _____

"Keep your face always toward the sunshine—
and, shadows will fall behind you."

—WALT WHITMAN

Thoughts from Your Soul

Gratitude to Fill Your Soul!

I AM THANKFUL FOR . . .   DATE _____

1. _____

2. _____

3. _____

I AM THANKFUL FOR . . .   DATE _____

1. _____

2. _____

3. _____

I AM THANKFUL FOR . . .   DATE _____

1. _____

2. _____

3 _____

*"You don't always need a plan. Sometimes you just need
to breathe, trust, let go, and see what happens."*

—MANDY HALE

Thoughts from Your Soul

Gratitude to Fill Your Soul!

I AM THANKFUL FOR . . .   DATE _____

1. _____

2. _____

3. _____

I AM THANKFUL FOR . . .   DATE _____

1. _____

2. _____

3. _____

I AM THANKFUL FOR . . .   DATE _____

1. _____

2. _____

3 _____

*"If you don't like something, change it. If you
can't change it, change your attitude."*

—MAYA ANGELOU

Thoughts from Your Soul

_____

_____

_____

_____

_____

_____

_____

_____

_____

_____

_____

_____

_____

_____

_____

_____

_____

_____

_____

_____

Gratitude to Fill Your Soul!

I AM THANKFUL FOR . . .   DATE _____

1. _____

2. _____

3. _____

I AM THANKFUL FOR . . .   DATE _____

1. _____

2. _____

3. _____

I AM THANKFUL FOR . . .   DATE _____

1. _____

2. _____

3 _____

"We can't solve our problems by the same thinking
we used when we created them."

—ALBERT EINSTEIN

Thoughts from Your Soul

Gratitude to Fill Your Soul!

I AM THANKFUL FOR . . .   DATE _____

1. _____

2. _____

3. _____

I AM THANKFUL FOR . . .   DATE _____

1. _____

2. _____

3. _____

I AM THANKFUL FOR . . .   DATE _____

1. _____

2. _____

3 _____

"You must be the change you wish you see in the world."

—GANDHI

Thoughts from Your Soul

Gratitude to Fill Your Soul!

I AM THANKFUL FOR . . .   DATE _____

1. _____

2. _____

3. _____

I AM THANKFUL FOR . . .   DATE _____

1. _____

2. _____

3. _____

I AM THANKFUL FOR . . .   DATE _____

1. _____

2. _____

3 _____

"How people treat you is their karma—
how you react is yours."

—Wayne Dyer

Thoughts from Your Soul

_____
_____
_____
_____
_____
_____
_____
_____
_____
_____
_____
_____
_____
_____
_____
_____
_____
_____
_____
_____
_____

Gratitude to Fill Your Soul!

I AM THANKFUL FOR . . .   DATE _____

1. _____

2. _____

3. _____

I AM THANKFUL FOR . . .   DATE _____

1. _____

2. _____

3. _____

I AM THANKFUL FOR . . .   DATE _____

1. _____

2. _____

3 _____

"The greatness of a man is not in how much wealth he acquires, but in his integrity and his ability to affect those around him positively."

—BOB MARLEY

Thoughts from Your Soul

Gratitude to Fill Your Soul!

I AM THANKFUL FOR . . . DATE _____

1. _____

2. _____

3. _____

I AM THANKFUL FOR . . . DATE _____

1. _____

2. _____

3. _____

I AM THANKFUL FOR . . . DATE _____

1. _____

2. _____

3 _____

"Life is like riding a bicycle. To keep your
balance, you must keep moving."

—Albert Einstein

Thoughts from Your Soul

Gratitude to Fill Your Soul!

I AM THANKFUL FOR . . .   DATE _____

1. _____

2. _____

3. _____

I AM THANKFUL FOR . . .   DATE _____

1. _____

2. _____

3. _____

I AM THANKFUL FOR . . .   DATE _____

1. _____

2. _____

3 _____

*"You can't go back and change the beginning, but you
can start where you are and change the ending."*

—C.S. Lewis

Thoughts from Your Soul

Gratitude to Fill Your Soul!

I AM THANKFUL FOR . . .   DATE _____

1. _____

2. _____

3. _____

I AM THANKFUL FOR . . .   DATE _____

1. _____

2. _____

3. _____

I AM THANKFUL FOR . . .   DATE _____

1. _____

2. _____

3 _____

"Only I can change my life—no one can do it for me."

—Carol Burnett

Thoughts from Your Soul

Gratitude to Fill Your Soul!

I AM THANKFUL FOR . . .   DATE _____

1. _____

2. _____

3. _____

I AM THANKFUL FOR . . .   DATE _____

1. _____

2. _____

3. _____

I AM THANKFUL FOR . . .   DATE _____

1. _____

2. _____

3 _____

"Nothing can dim the light that shines from within."

—Maya Angelou

Thoughts from Your Soul

Gratitude to Fill Your Soul!

I AM THANKFUL FOR . . .   DATE _____

1. _____

2. _____

3. _____

I AM THANKFUL FOR . . .   DATE _____

1. _____

2. _____

3. _____

I AM THANKFUL FOR . . .   DATE _____

1. _____

2. _____

3 _____

"Lead from the heart, not the head."

—Princess Diana

Thoughts from Your Soul

Gratitude to Fill Your Soul!

I AM THANKFUL FOR . . .   DATE

1.

2.

3.

I AM THANKFUL FOR . . .   DATE

1.

2.

3.

I AM THANKFUL FOR . . .   DATE

1.

2.

3

"If you want to awaken all of humanity, then awaken all of yourself.
If you want to eliminate the suffering in the world, then eliminate
all that is dark and negative in yourself. Truly, the greatest gift
you have to give is that of your own self-transformation."

—LAO TZU

Thoughts from Your Soul

Gratitude to Fill Your Soul!

I AM THANKFUL FOR . . .   DATE _____

1. _____

2. _____

3. _____

I AM THANKFUL FOR . . .   DATE _____

1. _____

2. _____

3. _____

I AM THANKFUL FOR . . .   DATE _____

1. _____

2. _____

3 _____

*"Everyday, think as you wake up, 'Today I am fortunate to have woken up.
I am alive, and have a precious human life. I am not going to waste it. I
am going to use all my energies to develop myself to expand my heart out
to others, and to achieve enlightenment for the benefit of all beings. I am
going to have kind thoughts toward others, I am not going to get angry, or
think badly about others. I am going to benefit others as much as I can.'"*

—DALAI LAMA

Thoughts from Your Soul

Thoughts from Your Soul

Made in the USA
Middletown, DE
18 September 2023

38694973R00109